THE ULTIMATE GUIDE

STOP PUTTING IT OFF!

WRITE YOUR BOOK
& PUBLISH IT

RISE2WRITE PUBLISHING LLC

ISBN: 9798340059406
Copyright © 2024 Rise2Write Publishing LLC
All rights reserved.
No part of this publication may be reproduced, stored in a retrieval system,
or transmitted in any form or by any means-for example, electronic,
photocopy, recording-without the prior written permission. The only
exceptions are brief quotations in printed reviews. Imprint: Independently
published.

RISE2WRITE PUBLISHING LLC
www.rise2write.com
rise2write@gmail.com

NEXT MONTH WRITING GOALS

GET ENOUGH SLEEP

HEALTH IS WEALTH

LOVE LIFE

BE FEARLESSLY AUTHENTIC

FEEL THE MOMENTS

CHERISH FAMILY PHOTOGRAPHS

STAY POSITIVE, BELIEVE IN YOURSELF

SELF AWARENESS

BE CURIOUS

NO REGRETS

RESEARCH

THE MORE WE TALK, THE MORE WE UNDERSTAND

JOT DOWN IDEAS

NO MORE EXCUSES!!!

TABLE OF
CONTENTS

STEPS TO TAKE BEFORE YOU BEGIN TO WRITE YOUR BOOK

- ## Create a Safe Writing Space

A quiet place where you are not distracted and can consistently focus on getting your writing done. Whether it's a home office, your couch, or a coffee shop, the environment where you work should allow you to focus, uninterrupted, for hours at a time.

- ## Decide on your book topic

Please make sure you think about what you want to write about.

What are you passionate about?
What area are you an expert in?
What is your vision for your book?
Write down all of your ideas.

EVERY WRITER HAS TO START FROM SOMEWHERE!

THE IMPORTANT TASK IS STARTING!!

- ## Gather all of your resources & tools

LET'S GET TO WRITING!

Whether you own a Mac or a PC, you will need to ensure that you have appropriate software access. To publish your book, you will need access to Microsoft Word since you'll need to submit Word document files.

THE 1ST STEP IN THE WRITING PROCESS

CHOOSE YOUR BOOK TOPIC

You can choose a topic you are passionate about or have expertise in. This will make the writing process more enjoyable and authentic.

BRAINSTORM & CREATE A LIST OF:
Key Moments of Inspiration
Key Moments of Learning
Challenges you Overcome
Things you are interested in
Areas in your life you would like to share
Areas you don't want to talk about
If you want to do a Fiction or Nonfiction
Transitional phases
Turning Points
Aha's
Solutions
Write down whatever else comes to mind!
Once you have released all of your ideas/thoughts.
It's time to narrow it down to your Book Topic & Genre.

There are over 35 Book Genres. Check out this Blog to learn more and narrow it down:
The Ultimate List of Book Genres: 35 Popular Genres, Explained

https://blog.reedsy.com/book-genres/

CHOOSE YOUR BOOK TOPIC & TITLE

Once your book topic is Finalized, you can create your book Title and determine which Category and genre it will fall under.

Now that you know what you'd like to write about, you can choose the book's title. Be Sure to Create a Meaningful Book Title. Do not feel too pressured to get the title right the first time; you may change it three more times.

Checklist for beginning to write:

Title of your Book:

Your vision:

Your Genre:

Estimated Size of Book: (6x9 is standard for fiction/nonfiction)

Here are Standard Size books for each different categories:

Trade: 5 ½" x 8 ½", 6" x 9"

Textbook: 5 ½" x 8 ½", 6" x 9", 7" x 10", 8.5" x 11"

Workbooks: 8 ½" x 11", 8" x 10"

Religious Books: 5 ½" x 8 ½", 6" x 9"

Science/Technical Books: 6" x 9", 7"x 10"

Childrens Book: 6" x 6", 6" x 8", 6" x 9", 8" x 10"

DO YOUR RESEARCH

Research is an essential tool for professional writers. If you're writing a non-fiction book, you'll likely want to spend time in libraries and archives, absorbing everything you can about your subject on Google or through purchased books.

Research is also helpful for fiction writers, as it can provide valuable context for the time or character archetypes you're writing about. It is also good to research Authors who have published similar content. What do you like about their book versus areas of improvement? That helps clarify the direction you want to take with your book.

Read books or listen to podcasts that cover subject matter similar to yours.

WRITING PROCESS: SET A WRITING SCHEDULE

ROUTINE HELPS REDUCE WRITERS BLOCK

Finding inspiration and staying creative.

You can set up a regular writing routine to make steady progress on your book. Consistency is key, whether it's a few hours each day or a dedicated block of time each week.

You can try setting daily word count targets to keep you on track. To hold yourself accountable, Schedule your writing time in your calendar so you won't skip it.

Ask a friend or fellow writer to hold you accountable as well by sending them updates on how much you've written that day and weekly.

Steps to Determine Your Finished Book Date:

1. *Decide on the total number of pages for your book (typically 150-250 pages).*
2. *Set the number of days per week you will write.*
3. *Divide the total pages by the number of writing days/weeks to estimate your completion date.*
   = DEADLINE DATE

THE 4TH STEP IN THE WRITING PROCESS

CREATE YOUR OUTLINE

Creating your outline is the most crucial step in the process. Create an outline for your book to organize your thoughts and ideas. This outline will serve as a roadmap for your writing and help you stay on track.

Outlining before writing your book is essential. Creating outlines helps your book content to flow. Outlines can be detailed chapter outlines or simple beat sheets in which each book section is plotted out.

They can be visual maps that serve as a graphic representation of where your book is headed. Regardless of your method, what's important is that you have a roadmap for your future writing sessions.

CLICK BELOW TO DOWNLOAD MY FREE OUTLINE TEMPLATE

https://rise2write.vip/

Steps to Creating your Story

Guidelines for Effective Writing:

Leverage your passion and expertise.

Address the reader's problems or dreams.

Ensure the topic is timely and relevant.

Create relatable characters.

01
CREATE YOUR CHARACTERS

Developing compelling characters.

Who is my main character?

Who would be your ideal reader? Age? Race? Gender? Religion? Income?

02
BUILD STRONG PLOT

Building a solid plot structure. Clarify your book's goal/message.

What kind of impact do you want to leave on the reader?

03 CREATE VIVID SETTINGS

Use sensory details: Describe sights, sounds, smells, tastes, and textures to immerse readers in the environment. Use figurative language: Use metaphors and similes to engage the reader's senses and evoke emotions.
Use all of your senses to describe your setting. What can you see? What can you hear? What can you smell? What can you taste? What can you feel? What can you taste? What can you feel?

04 CREATIVE DESCRIPTIVE SCENES

Use sensory details.
Choose specific and concrete words.
Use figurative language. Be the first to add your personal experience.

SECTION 1: Your STORY
SECTION 2: THE SITUATION
FINAL SECTION: THE SOLUTION

START WRITING

STICK TO YOUR WRITING ROUTINE

Start Writing! Do not worry about editing or formatting at this moment! Stick to your writing calendar while avoiding distractions such as Social Media, phone calls, etc. Research, outlining, and idea development are all critical steps at the beginning of your first book's writing journey, but there may come a time when preparation becomes procrastination.

At a certain point, it's time to begin writing your rough draft. This requires committing to consistent routines and productive writing habits. There are simple steps to maximize your chance for success, including just WRITING. TAKE MENTAL BREAKS WHEN NECESSARY!

SCAN THE QR CODE FOR *THE MANUSCRIPT TEMPLATE TO BEGIN WRITING ON*.

FINISH YOUR FIRST DRAFT

As you write your first draft, you'll encounter self-doubt, lack of motivation, and writer's block. That's normal. Try returning to your outline or research for inspiration whenever you feel stuck.

DO NOT ABANDON YOUR OUTLINE. STICK TO THE ORIGINAL PLAN TO SURE YOUR BOOK IS FLOWING WITH YOUR VISION. Try to manage your expectations.

The goal is for your first book to be a Bestselling book, but if not, that's okay. If you compare yourself to the success of others, you're doing your work a disservice. Focus on your story and being authentic. Do not apply unnecessary pressure on your writing.

Focus on writing until you reach the end of your story.

Please feel free to contact us, If you need Author Coaching Assistance.

EDIT & REVISE

Once you have completed the first draft, go back and revise it for clarity, coherence, and style. Take advantage of GRAMMARLY free app for the first round of edits: https://app.grammarly.com/ Do not do the Final Edits yourself! Consider seeking feedback from beta readers in Facebook/LinkedIn writing groups or editors to improve your manuscript.

Every good book goes through many rounds of revisions. You can endure the editing process or ask a friend or professional editor to help. Look for sentences that rely on cliché tropes or overly common descriptors. If you're writing fiction, try to determine where there are character inconsistencies, plot holes, or gaps in logic.

Develop a system to keep track of your edits.

Once you've finished your final draft of Editing, it's time to publish.

BOOK COVER DESIGN OPTIONS

DESIGN FOR PAPERBACK & HARDCOVER

HIRE A GRAPHIC DESIGNER

FIVERR

https://www.fiverr.com

BOOK BOLT

https://bookbolt.io/6641.html

No Content Book Research, Design, Listing

Here is why Book Bolt is essential in your low content publishing business

SAVE 20%: Coupon Code: Rise2write

CANVA FOR EBOOK DESIGNS

https://www.canva.com/book-covers/templates/

SELFPUB BOOKCOVERS

https://selfpubbookcovers.com

One-of-a-kind premade book covers where Authors can instantly customize and download their covers, and...

The LARGEST SELECTION of pre-made, professionally designed book covers for eBook and Print! Most covers start as low as $69.

PUBLISHING OPTIONS

SELF- PUBLISHING

1. You have to pay for editing, design, and marketing. You can save on printing if you choose a POD service.
2. You get around 60-70% of each book sold, depending on the online store you are selling in. Also, don't forget to pay your taxes.
3. You keep all your Rights. You are also responsible for purchasing the rights to all artwork you use.
4. You make all the decisions regarding your book. You might make good or bad decisions; nevertheless, they are your decisions.
5. It only depends on your time and abilities: your book can be on the shelves within months.
6. Everyone can get published. Your success depends on your market size and how well you can reach your target audience.
7. You can choose a distributor to distribute your book to major retailers and online bookstores worldwide.
8. The author has to take care of the publishing process and book promotion.

TRADITIONAL PUBLISHING

1. The publisher pays for everything, including printing and distribution.
2. You get around 10% of royalties after each book, depending on the publisher and the country.
3. The publisher has the rights to your book; the exact conditions depend on the publisher and the contract.
4. An expert team makes all the decisions regarding your book.
5. Publishing a book can take up to two years.
6. Only a selected few can get published. Publishers have limited funds and must choose from the incoming manuscripts. It is challenging to find a publisher that is willing to publish your book.
7. Publishers distribute their books all over the country.
8. The publisher takes care of the publishing process. You still have to take care of the book promotion after.

LET'S GET PUBLISHED

Pre-publication checklist

- **Customize or remove all placeholders.** Check one last time for remaining placeholder text.
- **Book details.** Does the information in your file (e.g., book title, author name) exactly match the book details you entered during title setup? Check your title page and headers to see if your information matches.
- **Images.** If you want to add images to your book, they should be high resolution. High resolution refers to the number of dots per inch (DPI) an image has. The more dots or pixels an image has, the clearer it will be. High-resolution images have at least 300 (DPI).
- **Legibility.** Can you easily read the text in your manuscript?
- The text should be in at least 10-point font, not cut off or overlapped by other elements. Also, make sure the text doesn't blend into the background. This may happen if the text and background colors are too similar.
- Save it in Microsoft Word for eBooks and PDF for print books.

DO NOT FORGET TO PROTECT YOUR HARD WORK:

1. PURCHASE AN ISBN FOR YOUR BOOK
2. COPYRIGHT YOUR BOOK

https://www.myidentifiers.com/identify-protect-your-book/registration-tools

Registration Tools

Register & Protect Your Book Identifiers from Bowker — including ISBNs, barcodes, and SANs — make book marketing and distribution more efficient for booksellers, libraries, universities, and

myidentifiers.com · Oct 1, 2019

LET'S GET PUBLISHED

SELF-PUBLISHING DISTRIBUTIONS OPTIONS FOR EBOOKS

1) *Amazon Kindle Direct Publishing (KDP):* Amazon KDP is a popular platform for publishing e-books in Kindle format. You can upload your e-book, set the price, and put it on the Kindle Store to make it available to a broad audience.

2) *Smashwords:* Smashwords allows you to create e-books in various file formats and distribute them in online bookstores such as Barnes & Noble, Kobo, and Apple Books.

3) *Lulu:* Lulu is a self-publishing platform that allows you to create, format, and publish e-books. They also offer distribution options in other online bookstores.

4) *Apple Books:* Apple Books is an e-book platform where you can publish your works and share them with a large audience. It is especially attractive to users of Apple devices.

5) Google Play Books: Google Play Books is a marketplace for e-books where you can sell your digital works. It is compatible with Android devices and reaches a wide user base.

6) *Barnes & Noble Nook Press:* Nook Press is Barnes & Noble's self-publishing platform, one of the largest book retailers in the US. Here you can upload and publish your e-books.

7) *Draft2Digital:* Draft2Digital is a platform that simplifies ebook distribution and offers tools for formatting, promotion, and sales tracking.

LET'S GET PUBLISHED
Print Books Self-Publishing Options:

1) *Amazon Kindle Direct Publishing (KDP)* Print-on-Demand (POD): With KDP, you can also create print books through their Print-on-Demand program. This means that books are not printed until an order is received. You can upload your book layout, design the cover, and put it up for sale.

2) *IngramSpark:* IngramSpark is a popular book printing and distribution service provider. You can upload your book layout, design the cover, and make it available for sale in various bookstores and online stores.

3) *Barnes & Noble Press:* Barnes & Noble Press offers the ability to create print books and sell them both online on their website and in select bookstores.

4) *Kobo Writing Life:* Kobo Writing Life is a self-publishing platform for e-books and print books that allows you to publish your work to their global network of booksellers and e-book readers.

5) *BookBaby:* BookBaby is a comprehensive self-publishing platform that offers services for creating and publishing print books. They support various book formats and offer printing and distribution services to sell your books in various channels.

6) *Blurb:* Blurb is a platform that allows authors to create and publish their own custom print books. They offer intuitive design software that allows you to design your book layout. Blurb also offers printing and distribution services to sell your books through their own website, Amazon, and other bookstores.

7) *Draft2Digital:* Gives you a fast, easy way to self-publish. They support the formatting. You set the price of your books, get monthly payments, and see daily reports of your book sales. They offer 24-hour support and dedicated customer service. They publish on multiple sites.

PUBLISHING RECOMMENDATION

AMAZON-KDP

https://kdp.amazon.com/en_US/help/topic/GHKDSCW2KQ3K4UU4

FORMATTING

https://youtu.be/kTkMUoxD2TU?si=cPi1l_PFesVZy5r8

BOOK COVER CREATION

https://youtu.be/QZj3MKxDB8A?si=QZqzqheR-lmdeOju

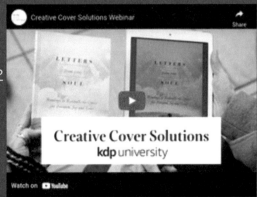

PUBLISHING
RECOMMENDATION

DRAFT2DIGITAL

https://www.draft2digital.com/authordevans

Draft2Digital

Your book is your priority. Our priority is you. We build tools and services that let you focus on writing while we take care of layout, publishing, distributi

https://youtu.be/zevfgrLVq90?si=oN9QskyEmYbIkPCO

https://www.youtube.com/live/3v7G8WItsP0?
si=ftkqqAgUbuxtP_1D

MARKET YOUR BOOK

Create a marketing plan to promote your book to your target audience. To promote your book, create an Author Page and a Digital shop. You can create a Free Author Page with my two Recommendations: Amazon and Draft2Digital.

You can create a digital shop with BEACONS.AI:
https://beacons.ai/signup?c=rise2write

The digital shop will promote your book with a direct link for purchase and could offer freebies, such as tips related to your topic.

It is important to build an author platform, engage with readers on social media, and seek reviews from book bloggers and influencers.

Writing a book begins your journey, so stay positive and persistent.

FREE SITES TO MARKET YOUR BOOK

http://www.kboards.com/

http://www.bookhitch.com/

http://www.booksie.com/

Scribd http://www.scribd.com

http://www.ebookforum.info

http://www.friends4brandt.com

http://www.bookgrouponline.com/forum

http://www.absolutewrite.com/forums

http://forums.onlinebookclub.org

http://www.bookandreader.com

http://thebookmarketingnetwork.com/forum

http://www.reading-forum.co.uk/forum

http://www.online-literature.com/forums

http://www.writing.com http://forums.onlinebookclub.org

http://smashwords.com

Scan the QR Code below to Access over 190 Facebook

Groups to market your book in.

WAYS TO MONETIZE YOUR BOOK

To fast track your income to six or
seven figures, add a program, product or service to your book.

- Order in bulk and sell at your Local events
- Create a course based on your Book
- Create a YouTube Channel based on your Book
- Create a Coaching Program
- Start a membership/community
- Digital Products
- Speaking engagements
- Book to 1:1 VIP clients
- Brand through Merchandize: Apparel, Coffee mugs, Tumblrs, etc.

THE BASIC STEPS OVERVIEW TO WRITING
YOUR FIRST BOOK

OUTLINE

1

Map your main idea, chapters, plot summaries and characters.

1ST DRAFT

2

Do your research, get into a routine and start writing your first draft.

EDITING

3

It's time to revise! If you're able, use a professional editor or ask a friend.

2ND DRAFT

4

Apply your edits, get the story and tone right, then cut what needs cutting!

PUBLISH

5

Submit a book proposal or self-publish your book out into the world!

Still need Help, Schedule a Call w/us:

SCAN QR CODE

ABOUT
RISE2WRITE PUBLISHING LLC

Rise2Write Publishing LLC is a full-service indie publishing company dedicated to empowering minority Children and Adults to become Published Authors.

Rise2Write Publishing LLC offers comprehensive book publishing services that guide clients through the entire publishing journey from inception to publication. Specializing in nonfiction, fiction, children's books, and more, we ensure a seamless and high-quality publishing experience. Our diverse services include ghostwriting, content creation, book layout, design, marketing, and author page creation. By leveraging our expertise, we help authors publish their books on 16+ top platforms, enabling them to retain 100% of their book royalties.

At Rise2Write Publishing LLC, our primary objective is to simplify the publishing process, allowing writers to concentrate on their craft.

If you are still feeling stuck, let us help you bring your book to life.

I PRAY THIS GUIDE WAS
HELPFUL & WISH YOU SUCCESS
ON YOUR FIRST BOOK!

THANK YOU

Contact us if you have any
question.

Email :   rise2write@gmail.com
Website :   www.rise2write.com
Digital Store: www.rise2write.vip

Made in the USA
Columbia, SC
23 December 2024

48165711R00031